THE LAND WILL HOLD YOU

For my parents,
Peter and Colleen Logue

Also by Mary Walker

Lullaby for Mothers: motherhood in poems

FROM READERS OF *LULLABY FOR MOTHERS*

"There is deep healing and promise here for the journey ahead, no matter your age."~ *Lisa Creech Bledsoe, author of Appalachian Ground and Wolf Laundry*

"I go to bed most nights with Lullaby for Mothers by my side and it has been such soul medicine for me." ~ *Emily Bagaric*

"This is uplifting, healing and nurturing." ~ *Anja Mohn-Mitchell*

"I wish all mothers could read this soulful book of poems. Having them on your countertop and reading one in the midst of a busy day might just transform how you experience what comes next." ~ *Marion Rose Ph.D.*

"This little poetry book is a gem. My mum loves hers already. What a fabulous gift for right now." ~ *Lisa Markwick*

"Mary has a way of quickly transporting her reader right into her worlds, inner and outer, through her vivid and touching poetry." ~ *Lauren Oujiri*

"Such a divine and pleasurable read." ~ *Krystal Cook*

"Mary unites the eternal voice of Mother Earth, of the divine, and of unconditional love with the extraordinary specificity of her own being, bringing universal ideas to life." ~ *Naina Saligram*

"Mary's poetry is a sweet light guiding us home. Her words have changed the relationship I have with my children, with myself as a mother, and with my own mother, in the most beautiful way." ~ *Annie Ferguson Muscato*

"I sometimes wonder if Mary has snuck into my soul and stolen her words from me." ~ *Melissa Joseph Thorn*

"Mary's poetry is breathtakingly beautiful." ~ *Jean Bonnitcha*

THE LAND WILL HOLD YOU

MARY WALKER

First published in New Zealand 2022
Castle Press
PO Box 47165
Upper Hutt 5143
New Zealand

Copyright © Mary Walker 2022

Published in New Zealand 2022

Cover design: Sara Gaspar
Cover painting: Earth (2021), by Jane Blackmore
Book interior: Sophie White
Author Photo: © Amber-Jayne Bain

All rights reserved. No part of this publication may be reproduced, stored in a retrieval system, or transmitted, in any form or by any means without the prior written permission of the publisher, nor be otherwise circulated in any form of binding or cover other than that in which it is published and without a similar condition being imposed on the subsequent purchaser.

A catalogue record is available at the National Library of New Zealand.

ISBN: 978-0-473-59315-5 (paperback)
ISBN: 978-0-473-59316-2 (hardback)

Printed by Ingram Spark

CONTENTS

Preface	11
Precognition	13
Intuit	14
What Beckons	15
Flood	16
The Heart Of Fear	17
Unfurl	18
Landform	19
Breach	20
Landslide	21
Still	22
Trust	23
Let It Out	24
Spells	25
Sunrise	26
The Veil	27
A Prayer For Belonging	28
Ground	29
At The Shore	30
Fabric	31
An Early Morning	32
How To Find Things	33
Wild Fruit	34
Speak	35
I, River	36
Tides	37
Belonging	38
Found	39
Thirst	40
Faith	41
Rain	42
On The First Warm Day	43

The Broken And The Whole	44
New Ground	45
The Edge	46
Mist	47
Float	48
Downpour	49
Tectonic	50
Mountain	51
More Than We Can Grasp	52
Wellspring	53
Inexplicable	54
Weather	55
Knowing	56
Incomplete	57
Let Go	58
The Forest	59
Guardian	60
Repair	61
Thrive	62
Restore	63
Fever	64
The Answer	65
Walk Gently	66
Solstice	67
When Busy	68
Feathers	69
Spring Song	70
Supple	72
Tend	73
When The Web Breaks	74
The Beginner	75
Acknowledgements	77

PREFACE

Less concrete underfoot, more stars overhead. The thought arrived out of nowhere. It was Saturday morning, and I had just sat down at my favourite inner city cafe for brunch. What prompted the thought, I do not know. But it set in motion a chain of events that led me out of the city and onto the land I now call home.

My childhood had been spent on a farm at the foot of the Tararua Ranges in New Zealand. A state highway ran up the centre of Wairarapa's great rural plain. Small towns were strung along the highway like beads on a chain. Between the clusters of houses, shops and schools lay great stretches of land, with a great big sky overhead. School and sleepovers and part-time jobs lay in town. But home was paddocks and pine trees and wide open space.

At 17 I headed to the city for university and stayed for the career. After fifteen years of city living, the life force of the land that had once sustained me ran dry. Like a fallen tree whose branches can only drink from the trunk for so long, I needed replenishing. I needed to reroot. *Less concrete underfoot, more stars overhead.*

The story of how I came to live where I do is charmed, and for another time. But why I was drawn here—what lay in store for me as a result—is contained in these poems.

Many of us feel the land, and feel like we hear her speak. It feels strange to say that out loud, which is a shame and, to my mind, at the heart of our ecological crisis. We've wandered far from what sustains us. Many of us know the way back, but it's frightening to peel away from the crowd. A way of living and being that surely once was innate now requires courage to reestablish.

This book is for anyone who loves the land and wants to go deeper, fall harder, and stray further. It's for those who love the Earth and long to hear her speak back. May it provide some sustenance for the journey ahead.

PRECOGNITION

The sun inches across the land,
rays spreading over the turning earth.
We wake into a day
already alive and waiting,
into a life already pregnant
with the thought of us,
preceding ourselves
as the sun's light precedes the day.

INTUIT

There are places where thoughts cannot go,
places your mind will not take you,
like a road that stops at the foot of a hill
or falls short in the deep of a valley.

Be free of mind and digressions.
Shrug off worries and plans,
set aside intent,
throw down the map you think
got you this far.

Where the road runs out, explore.
Go by feel, by taste,
by your quivering skin.
Let the body lead.
This way, your bones sing,
this way home.

WHAT BECKONS

Come to the place
where your lane meets stream and hedgerow,

just beyond the gate of yourself,
where you tip from gardened to wild.

Come to the place
through which all things pass and none stay.

Follow the hoof prints
down the mud-thick lane.

Slide under the brambly hedge.
Let it take the clothes from your back.

Spill into the creek and join the leaves
fallen and flowing home at last.

Come to the place that wants to change you.
Be daring as you leave it.

FLOOD

Sometimes you need to rise
and sometimes
you must flood.

Go ahead—
press the edges.
Spread out.

Wash clear the margins
where almost, not quite,
and maybe took root.

Alter the boundaries.
Carve something new
with your life-giving self.

Be the deluge,
be the ark—
the land can take all that you've got.

THE HEART OF FEAR

In the heart of fear lies fearlessness.
In the eye of the hurricane stillness presides.
Nothing can wipe out your centre,
that axis on which your world turns.

Here, blue sky reigns and quiet travels with you.
To reside here is not to deny the storm,
but to see its lashing rain, witness its violent strength
and feel peace, still.

UNFURL

A steady eye can see it,
the way a cloud blossoms
from its centre,
opening from the inside.

It's simple—
open the valve to your truest part,
feel it fill and move you,
let what is inside, out.

Doesn't it look easy?
Can't you imagine floating?

Yet even while unfurling the cloud is ending—
wind pulling its tail,
air eating at its edges.
Death is at the door from the start.

In this space between earth and sky,
between the here and almost-not,
what moves you?
What will you come apart for?

Knowing nothing of such choices,
the clouds watch on,
effortlessly
expanding anyway.

LANDFORM

Every landform holds within
the story of how it came to be.
We each have our bedrock,
shifting layers of sand or shale,
gravel, clay, igneous rock,
some, ash.
Learn your layers,
read your striations
like lines in a book.
The forces that shaped you—
eruption, fire, gentle breeze—
they brought you here,
they made you.
None of us are spared the elements.
We all break down, refine
and still change comes,
the story writes on—
a landform is never finished.

BREACH

When who you are comes on fast,
as if the side of you was punctured with a nail,
and the sheer weight of your unlived life,
the grand reservoir that is you,
explodes out in a torrent,

when you realise you are a rushing river,
a splendid waterfall,
that you were never a stagnant pool,
never meant to be dammed,

will you realise that which you avoided
released you in the end?
Now that you are the ocean,
will you know you were also the nail?

LANDSLIDE

Don't you long to let go?
Uncurl those cramped fingers
and loosen your grip on life.
Let go the rules you cling to
and ride the rattling scree.
What do you think might happen
besides falling?
What do you worry you'll feel
besides relief?
The drop is shorter than you think,
the gap between control and freedom
less than the width of a hair.
The gravel you churn with your fear
gives way to alpine moss;
the relief, immediate and soft.

STILL

Stay a while, still.
Less like the wind,
more like the ground you stand on.
Where are you going anyway?
and what for? and must you?

The Earth moves only as needed
toward nourishment,
toward light,
toward life.
Move toward what matters.

TRUST

We long to see the hand of the invisible,
look for evidence under every rock,
lift edges and corners of happenings
in the hope that we will catch it.
We feel it under the skin of life,
a tremor below the surface,
and though we know it, we don't trust it,
though we feel it, we want to see it,
though we cry *show me!*
we turn away from every sign.

LET IT OUT

I know you think it will kill you.
I know you don't say that lightly.

Whatever it is—
the mountain you face,
the cliff edge you stand on,
the moving wall of water
before which you are always, only
one step ahead—

I know it seems impossible,
that what you're sure will kill you
will actually set you free

but, the mountain bows down,
the cliff commands the beach
to rise and meet your feet,
the wall of water pursues you
only so it can carry you home.

All you hold at bay is yourself.
All that might die is the thought
I must hold this in.

SPELLS

Too late in the morning
to go unseen,
a deer roars.
Without thinking
I press my finger to my lips,
casting a cloak over it,
the way I cast spells
over each tall tree still standing,
and my children while they sleep.

SUNRISE

A thin line of cloud
on the lip of the hill
slides down into the valley,
running ahead of the sun's warmth
as if chased by it,
as if afraid,
and I wonder
why we do that,
why we run from the light.

THE VEIL

When the wind shifts the curtain,
when the veil slips aside
and all is seen as light and air

life is coloured golden for a moment,
and you are the breeze and the land,
you are the sun that never sets.

A PRAYER FOR BELONGING

If I travel, let me feel every footstep.
Let me know myself as that through which I pass.

If I stay, let me belong to the land I stand on.
Let me be here in my life.

GROUND

Go to the earth
to ground,
to lay down,
place down
all the things
you cannot carry.

AT THE SHORE

I don't know this language.
I don't know how the rounded pebbles got here,
which rocks were ground down
to make this clay-coloured sand.
Did these leathery leaves blow or wash up here?
How long till the tide takes the seaweed again?
Whose are these feathers,
who burrows in the sand,
what swims ten feet out in the water?

Someone loves this beach and is known by it
for the press of their foot, by the skin
the sand sloughs off and mixes with its own.
Someone belongs here, cries here, reads the wind,
knows it by wave and swell.
Someone mingles themselves with this sea,
blesses themselves with this water.
What a love,
to love a place.

FABRIC

We are each the fine end
of not just one but many lines.
Not just two, but four, eight, sixteen,
thirty-two ply and more.

We are a skein of threads,
our needle poised over a land
which lies like fabric inert
but it, too, is it's own end point—

the latest in a long line of mountains,
valley, daughter of all valleys
laid down before her,
a river ever running,
a knot of trees, weaving its thread
since it first broke ground.

And in our every footstep
these two points meet,
our hands and land pressing, seaming,
our every life streaming
behind us.

AN EARLY MORNING

When gifted an early morning,
when something wakes you,
holds you in its pre-dawn hand
and will not let you go,
here is what it's not—
it's not for getting a jump on things,
not for ticking more off the list,
for squeezing more in or wringing more out
of your already spoken-for day.

When gifted an early morning
take in the dawn chorus,
see what it means to wake alive and expectant,
notice the birds quieten as the sky lightens,
see the first flush of light on the underside of clouds,
see them pink and blush mauve
and fall away grey.

See how the birds shift gear,
now feeding, now preening,
now landing in trees
like brooches pinned to a shawl.
Be surprised by a second flush of sunrise,
by the sun cresting the hill, by the clouds
warm and golden in the early morning.

HOW TO FIND THINGS

Go early.
Flush blackbirds from bushes,
let the cat find warm trails
of hedgehog, pukeko, quail.
Be mindful of hedgerows, fringe dwellers,
dream keepers sweeping night clear for day.
See the dew settled on the grass,
the lawn adorned with spiderwebs.

See your nose, pinked,
your breath in small clouds,
your fingers numbing.
Go where you flow,
expecting nothing but joy.
Let it be enough—
this one fallen leaf,
one stem of grass,
one blackberry, chilled
overnight in earth's larder.

WILD FRUIT

Beyond my garden fence,
weeds are simply plants.
I might rip blackberry from my borders,
but I covet its fruit in the wild.

You may not fit where you are:
too big for small spaces,
too loose for tight boundaries,
too loud, too colourful,
too new.

Over the fence,
the world is hungry for you;
you belong, out there.
Arch your canes over the gate,
beg the birds to lift you.
However you do it,
go free.

SPEAK

Between the earth and the air above
life speaks in clouds.
Converse with your maker,
lean across your sky.
Paint your desire in feathered script,
speak it to rivers, call over foothills,
pour across plains, cry
return me to the sea!
Hear the river reply
I'll carry you home.

I, RIVER

Every river has its life.
The young, sinuous,
carving and sculpting rocks,
rushing forward in waterfalls,
haste, haste,
grit and hurry.

It is not will
that carries me now, but trust
and the ocean's deep call.
In the opening out of a life
time expands and lands unfold,
bowing, allowing me through.

I lay back and trust.
Like water, I find my own level.
Cupped in Earth's hands,
I cover fathoms
with no effort at all.
Watch now as I braid this land.
Listen, I sing of the sea.

TIDES

A spring tide inches and ebbs like any other—
easy to ignore until you're up to your ankles in it.
It follows the rules of regular tides
but breaks the one we trust the most:
this is where the sea stops | this is where land begins.

Yesterday we trod here without thought.
Today we're swamped and cannot see the ground.
The edge of us feels threatened, but then,
our contours were always a fiction.

The tide will recede, as it always does.
Life will resume its usual ebb, its usual flow.
Land remains, as ever.

BELONGING

You love this place, but like a stranger,
as if you are intruding on the earth's great peace.
It's one thing to be reverent,
another to live on bent knee.
Do not apologise
as if your presence diminishes the space.
You belong to it
as the stone belongs to the creek,
the fern to the fallen beech,
the epiphyte to air.
We are all ephemera, all essential,
on this land and of it.

FOUND

You don't need to mine,
you don't need to tunnel for
or root out anything.
Your vast soul,
that seabed on which
the ocean of you rests,
holds every part of you,
holds you like coral to a reef,
releasing filaments,
strands of memory,
laced treasure
to rise and float,
to make its way to the shore
of your attention,
and, naturally, be found.

THIRST

Our river runs a lifetime
though the water each moment is new.
Chasing what the current carries from us,
whether for love or despair,
is to miss the only water
we ever need—

singing over stones at our feet,
laughing and lapping at our ankles,
water we can cup, raise to our
mouth and drink.
Longing for what has passed
or what might come
will only leave us thirsty.

FAITH

We don't need to know
how or when or why,
only that the waves will carry us,
gentle hands passing us
all the way to shore.

RAIN

I know you're tired,
lurching from one exhausted moment
to the next, rushed
through life
like a cloud
at the mercy of the wind.

It's a relief, isn't it,
to let go, let out
what weighs heavy on your heart;
to lie on the shoulder of the hill
and weep.

You're not asked to hold it all.
Life invites release,
places mountains in your path
to clear the skies
and water
all that you watch over.

What the cloud never sees
is that the valley floor blooms
after rain.

ON THE FIRST WARM DAY

Take off your shoes,
hang out the sheets,
see the snow on the mountain, melting.
The blades of grass bow down
for your feet,
the damp earth
gives as you walk.
See the air catch the blanket, billow
and settle. Lie down.

Let the newborn sun warm your cheek,
watch the honeybees move
from flower to flower
quilting the lawn.
Brush the thyme, hot and stony,
promising summer,
the geranium, thick with rose,
clove and pepper.

Suspended in the tree
is a clutch of blue eggs
and the lilac is in bud.
Take the sheets from the line,
breeze in their fibres,
eat the sweet grass,
pocket the leaf,
press spring into every fold.

THE BROKEN AND THE WHOLE

To be able to swallow the broken
we must feast on what is still whole—
taste the air, not just gulp it,
enjoy the apple-scented rose
having its strange winter flush,
savour a childish delight in mud
even as the waters rise.

For every fear, allow pleasure,
a heedless, senseless pleasure
in whatever it is you love.
Revel in the certainties—
the rising sun,
the moon pulling the tides,
the ones you love
and are loved by.

Allow joy and worry in equal measure,
and keep the proportions in check.
A cook knows to double all parts
not just some—
as much liquid as dry,
extra sweet to balance the salt—
a widened pan to hold it all,
the broken and the whole.

NEW GROUND

A river will bite at the bank that bars its way.
Backed up against the wall of itself,
like our own self welling up,
it insists on change.

The gentle shuffle of stones
and spreading of sand is replaced with
energy hurled at the sides
of an outgrown self.

It can look and feel violent
to protest the bank,
to press back on that which blocks us,
but do not judge.

Whatever the river does,
whether push, rush, rest, or glide,
never will it condemn itself
for carving out new ground.

THE EDGE

I love your broken edges,
the way you spill into the sea,
with your stalwart cliffs eroding,
you are beautiful.
Allow your collected stories
to tumble on the shore,
wearing corners, softening edges,
becoming treasure.
Under the watch of the headland,
weigh the past in the palm of your hand.
Keep the good for the memory box,
gift the rest to the sea.

MIST

The mountains are gone.
With the long view hidden, the vast mid-ground,
the great swathe of our days, now looms.

What was indistinct comes clear.
The shapes of things closer to home appear.
The trees across the way are sharp, alive and talking.

Memories hidden in branches have language again,
fly straight at me, banking at the last
before curling back on themselves,

reaching the trees as the sun rises, and the mist lifts.
Memories fade as the mountain appears,
returning yesterday to its folds.

FLOAT

To stay afloat
you must set aside praying
and save yourself.
You must do the thing
you think you cannot do—
press your head back
and further back still,
offering to the water
the part of you that breathes.
Lift your body to the surface
and give it to the air
which cannot carry you,
at least, not alone.

In that thin slice,
there on the surface
where air and water meet,
you'll find yourself
in the unlikely position
of being held,
clasped between two hands,
as it were, in prayer.

DOWNPOUR

So long dry,
the land seems to have forgotten
what to do with all the wet,
seems to lay back and give up,
letting the water have its way.

Silently and out of sight
it takes what it can.
The water, too, does its bit,
leaning into downhill pulls, carving hollows,
allowing the land to take abundance,
one sip at a time.

It's like that at first,
going from drought to drowning,
though no one yet has perished
under the weight of too much good.

TECTONIC

You could say we are adrift
but only if we were separate.
You could fear the random ruptures
or see the land answering its own call.
The solid ground you walk on rides a mantle,
moved by its own shapeless heat.
There is fire in the belly.

You boil with an urge to express
and a heat that cares nothing
for your tidy arrangements.
Land reinvents itself, rising up,
creating new places to stand,
taking down the old—
the known sacrificed for the new
again and again.

Secure your life as much as you like,
take a snapshot.
Today's landscape is no match for your burning core.
Your past is no match for the mountain.

MOUNTAIN

I am not finite.
I am not a pretty postcard.
I am solid, but wear as you watch.
Time shakes me loose,
and I shake things loose,
and I choose to let things fall.
When the ground falters
watch me bow, watch me rise
watch me change before your eyes.
I am not finite, I am flux
and I am not finished yet.

MORE THAN WE CAN GRASP

There is more here than can be grasped in two hands,
a world too large to throw our arms around.

Everything—the lone cricket singing in the tall rye grass,
one falling feather, a single stripped bone—

everything contains everything else.
Each is a well into which we could fall.

Every day the world begs—stand face to face with its creatures.
This blade of grass, not the sea from which you pluck it,

this head of clover, not the nine with which it sways,
this one bird, singing to you in the dead of night.

WELLSPRING

She does not judge the form it takes,
she cares not for its language.
She flows like water
and will find her way through
in the end.
She doesn't mind the depth
or the distance she must travel,
sees no obstacle that can't be moved
or worn smooth.
Hers is a constant spring
and she will quench your thirst.
Drink and drink again.

INEXPLICABLE

Nothing is for nothing.
Everything a branch,
an expression of that to which it belongs.
Everything makes sense
when seen connected.
No aberrations, no missteps,
the inexplicable has its place.

WEATHER

It's easy to love life under blue skies,
arms thrown wide to the weather,
the sun shining, highlighting
life's soft curves.

Who are you when the clouds come?
Who are you in the rain?
Where does loss hide,
where does the hurt pool
unable to find its way home?

The earth may take the rain in time
and storms are only passing through.
Still, things can be done—
pain unearthed,
your life, aerated,
wounds and aches
brought home to light.

Land has its natural balance
and you have yours.
A loving state,
able to welcome the rain.

KNOWING

Like the full moon rising
whole and complete,
all at once, we know.
We may think we worked it out,
show a logic that proves it,
point to the pulleys and levers
that hauled this new surety
into the sky,
but that isn't how this works.

It arrives
and we receive it
gifted, wrapped and ready,
held up by a hand in the night.

If we could do it—
receive with grace what is given
without busying ourselves
in the name of deserving—
if we trusted that what is true
will arrive with beauty and ease,
what might we know,
what might we love,
what might we choose to let go?

INCOMPLETE

Like mountains
driven up, eroded,
every day we rise
and fall back down.

Emerging in space
and time,
releasing the past
for something new.

Always arriving
and on the way out,
Always perfect,
always incomplete.

LET GO

It's easy to feel love for the dawning,
to be awed by our incoming light

but as the new rises, so does the old set.
What is it that wants to let go?

THE FOREST

There is no substitute
for feeling what calls to be felt,
no shortcut through the forest.

Each tree an experience,
each interaction, its own fall of light,
the ground itself littered with things
that ask to be known by name.

It's not just loss
that hides in the undergrowth, but joy,
and suppressed and dampened hopes.

The forest is alive with all that you are.
Hush now, listen.

GUARDIAN

The idea is appealing.
With one clean cut
you could rise up in a new life.

It's tempting
to slice through the undergrowth,
concrete the marsh,
to level the uneven.

Hold on—
this is not just swamp you tread—
this is fallen forest,
rich with the seeds of your life to come.
Let it emerge softly.
Look for an opening—
a gap between trees,
where the light falls, playing,
inviting you in.

Put down the scythe—
go gently, let the clearing appear.
Love yourself as land,
and see how you grow.

REPAIR

So it comes away in layers,
flakes and falls like bark.
Not the single slice you hoped for,
not that clean start you wanted
which, anyway, is another kind of violence.

It is a sloughing, natural,
a steady easy shed of things let go.
The wind will shift some,
lift the light unwanted,
and the ground will shake some down

but mostly it's the returning.
It's the coming back that does it,
time and again to the foot of the tree,
to hear its song, to witness the fall
to feel your sap rise in spring.

THRIVE

Pasture covered slopes will slip,
shallow rooted grass
cannot hold a hill on its own.
A life stripped of riches,
a self swept aside
for blending in
barely holds itself together.
You are a forest,
wild and diverse.
Let new ideas take root,
let colour bloom,
let the strange and exotic spring up.
Recolonise your life.

RESTORE

It seems sudden, but isn't,
the overwintered bulbs
that rise from the ground overnight.

Flowering is their shortest stop,
a visible high point
in the arc of a life—

soaking up the sun before the trees come into leaf,
storing reserves, thickening the bulb
on which everything depends.

We treasure the flowers but truth is their gift—
to bloom without replenishment
shortens a life.

FEVER

Long before
the autumn rains,
the settled dew greens
the land's grazed face.

Mother
lifts our fevered head,
offering one small spoon
at a time.

It is the air itself
that saves us.
Night's cool cover, a cloth
on our burning face.

We long for a downpour
forgetting
we need only a little, often.

One teaspoon of mercy.
One well-timed act of grace.

THE ANSWER

The trees have nothing to say, and the ryegrass is mute.
Below me, the creek speaks only to the mudfish, the watercress,
the dragonfly nymph.

This ladybird crossing the back of my hand could be heralding
good wishes or taking the direct route home. Either way, it does
not say.

And who knows what the stones are doing. This one here I nudge
with my boot. This greywacke stone—wrenched from the ground,
split, tumbled, and left to lie—it has seen it all and is
the least likely to tell.

Still, I listen. I strain my ears until the tendons in my neck are
strung like wire. Something could burst. How do we live with
silence? Glad, but unanswered, is one way. It could be enough.

Yet, right now aren't people all over giving thanks for what they
read in the water and the wind-bent pines? Aren't I sunning
myself, closed-eyed on this mossed trunk, moved to name the
sounds I cannot hear?

Didn't I stand here two nights ago, head thrown back to see
the crescent moon, Jupiter hanging from its lip as if from a string,
as if falling from the moon's cup; the night air settling on my face
and a heron flying over me, stitching me into this place yet again?

You love this place and your small part in it. Silence one day,
the next, your name carved in the trunk of its tree like a lover.

WALK GENTLY

Slow down.
Press lightly with your feet.
Shoes on, shoes off, it doesn't matter.
The land just wants to hold you.

Feel the air
brush your cheeks as you go,
welcoming your breath,
folding it back into itself

even as it rushes to fill you again,
settling in the cup of your ear,
in the space between lashes,
running, like a hand, over your hair.

SOLSTICE

On your darkest day,
your shadow long on the ground,
despair running full length,
depths scraped bare,
lungs desperate
for air, remember

the deepest point of winter
is the shortest stop of all.
It is but a moment,
an axis on which
your spring
and autumn
turn.

Feel for the point
of your longest night,
trace every shadow,
look for the place
where shadow retreats
and upswing begins.

WHEN BUSY

The hawk spins on one wing
like a skater on ice, inviting me to look.
The kereru whistles past my window
and fondly turns its head to see if I am watching.
I am not. I am lost.

A lamb is crying day and night.
Blackbirds face off in the stalls,
clicking their beaks,
banging breasts in mid-air
like stags in heat.

What could matter more than this?
This parade of spring, this string of moments
rising like pockets of air to the surface of a lake?
Where am I if not here to see this happen?
Where is it we go, and why?

I slip out the door.
The grass greets me like a friend.
A quail uncoils its song for me.
The hawk spins again in case I missed it.

FEATHERS

Each day I tread the same worn path,
though no bird flies over the same way twice,
the bees attend different flowers,
cicadas sing where yesterday there were none
and the hawk is scanning new trees.

A feather lies in wait for me,
having fallen from the sky.
No other will fall in quite the same way,
from that height to this spot
to be caught between two heads of rye.
The land looks the same
but is different in a thousand small ways.

We can think one day is much like another,
that we still are who we were before.
Or we can let ourselves be changed.
What looks familiar is not.
We are as new as the world we see.
Be delighted, be surprised.
Expect feathers.

SPRING SONG

The first lines of spring
are now long forgotten,
hidden in the blinding green,
lost in the flurry of life's business.
The first daffodil,
kingfisher call,
thick leaf buds,
all gone.
The first day without fire,
without cardigan, shoes,
folded away
in the envelope
marked *spring*.

Page two reads
clover up to the knee,
a racket of birds,
everything speckled,
unfurling.
First roses,
lilac-scented wind,
blossom fall.
The cuckoo is back,
the rhubarb up,
the hedgehog is awake
and stretching

and still spring writes on,
pages three, four and more,
shedding parchment
like petals, like leaves.

SUPPLE

An east wind blows
and it is not so much ill, as interesting,
creating fresh garden shapes,
revealing new vistas.

There's something different about you
I call to the trees,
as if to a friend
who cut her hair.

Branches sweep up and over,
leaves reveal their underside,
the whole garden bows,
as if honouring some new truth.

The world looks awry.
There is sky in new places,
curves of hill I've never seen before.
Whatever you've done, I like it!

Strange winds blow from time to time,
turning us to face the unseen,
new places, new horizons,
how supple we are as we bend.

TEND

I gather fallen limbs,
handle brittle lichened bones
with reverence,
returning them
to the base of their tree.
It is a privilege to warm the cloth,
to clean the hands of a child,
to wipe the face of a loved one
who can no longer.
I tend to the dying tree
knowing one day
this will be me.
When I cannot
hold the spoon to my own mouth,
when the soup spills,
when I am spilling over
and my body no longer
contains me,
may someone hold me,
hold the cup to my lips,
hold the paper to my pen,
hold me while I fall.

WHEN THE WEB BREAKS

When the web breaks,
when the threads, pulled too taut,
thin and thin,

when they can hold no more,
when they let go, resisting nothing,
and sigh, relieved

what was full, empties,
what was sure, becomes a question,
what was finished
begins again.

THE BEGINNER

Oh, to be spring again,
arriving in a world
wet, green, and electric.
To throw yourself
at the unknown,
to stand on new legs
in a wide field,
wobbly, but there.
To know nothing of the world
but what you encounter
each moment,
to have only instinct,
no default—
what a thrill!
What a thrill to be new
over and over
in one life.

ACKNOWLEDGEMENTS

These poems were published online before being brought together in this collection. My thanks to all those who read, responded to, and shared my poems over the last few years. Thank you for your support and friendship. It's a pleasure to walk alongside you.

Thank you to the people that helped bring this book to life—Sara Gaspar, Amanda Spedding, Sophie White and Rob Cranna.

Thanks to Jane Blackmore, whose painting *Earth* is featured on the cover. It contributes so much to the energy of this collection.

Special thanks to my family—to Hamish for his love and encouragement, and to my children who remind me what it means to live on purpose, and in peace.

Thanks, as always, to Mum and Dad who showed me that ideas can be trusted and dreams are there to be realised.

MARY WALKER was born in Aotearoa New Zealand to a Kiwi mother and Irish father. She lives with her husband and children in Te Awa Kairangi ki Uta / Upper Hutt.

As well as writing, Mary supports others to pursue creative lives through her online communities and workshops.

Lullaby for Mothers: motherhood in poems was her first book of poetry.

Visit Mary's website to join her free email poetry subscription, *A Beautiful Beginning*.

www.marywalker.co.nz

www.ingramcontent.com/pod-product-compliance
Lightning Source LLC
Chambersburg PA
CBHW022021290426
44109CB00015B/1262